Growing Trees

Written by **Judith Bauer Stamper**
Illustrated by **Wesley Lowe**

TeachingStrategies™ • Washington D.C.

For Teaching Strategies, Inc.
Publisher: Larry Bram
Editorial Director: Hilary Parrish Nelson
VP Curriculum and Assessment: Cate Heroman
Product Manager: Kai-leé Berke
Book Development Team: Sherrie Rudick and Jan Greenberg
Project Manager: Jo A. Wilson

For Q2AMedia
Editorial Director: Bonnie Dobkin
Editor and Curriculum Adviser: Suzanne Barchers
Program Manager: Gayatri Singh
Creative Director: Simmi Sikka
Project Manager: Santosh Vasudevan
Illustrator: Wesley Lowe
Designer: Ritu Chopra

Teaching Strategies, Inc.
P.O. Box 42243
Washington, DC 20015
www.TeachingStrategies.com

ISBN: 978-1-60617-127-1

Library of Congress Cataloging-in-Publication Data
Stamper, Judith Bauer.
  Growing trees / written by Judith Bauer Stamper ; illustrated by Wesley Lowe.
    p. cm.
  ISBN 978-1-60617-127-1
  1. Tree planting--Juvenile literature. 2. Trees--Juvenile literature. 3. Trees--Seedlings--
  Juvenile literature. I. Lowe, Wesley, ill. II. Title.
  SB435.S73 2010
  635.9'77--dc22
                              2009036909

CPSIA tracking label information:
RR Donnelley, Shenzhen, China
Date of Production: February 2011
Cohort: Batch 2

Printed and bound in China

2 3 4 5 6 7 8 9 10	15 14 13 12 11
Printing	Year Printed

This is a picture
of my tree and me.
We've been growing
up together for
a whole year.

It all began last summer. I went to visit
a national forest with my mom and dad.
A forest is a great place to learn about
trees. There are trees as far as you can see.

We took a hike with a forester, an expert on taking care of trees in the wild.

The forester showed us small, young trees and big, old trees that were like towering giants.

Then he explained the life cycle of a tree. It all starts out with a seed. In the spring, the warm sun makes the seed germinate, or begin to grow.

The seed sprouts a small root that grows down into the ground. The root absorbs water and minerals from the soil.

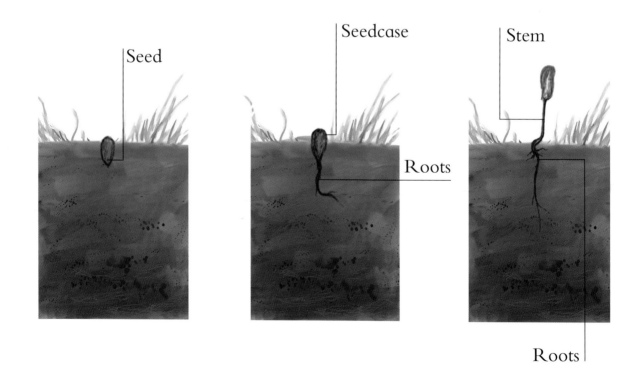

Seed

Seedcase

Stem

Roots

Roots

Next, a small stem pushes up out of the ground and grows two tiny seed leaves. The leaves use sunlight to give the tree energy to grow.

A new growth, called a shoot, appears at the tip of the stem. Larger leaves grow from the shoot. The seedling is on its way to becoming a tree.

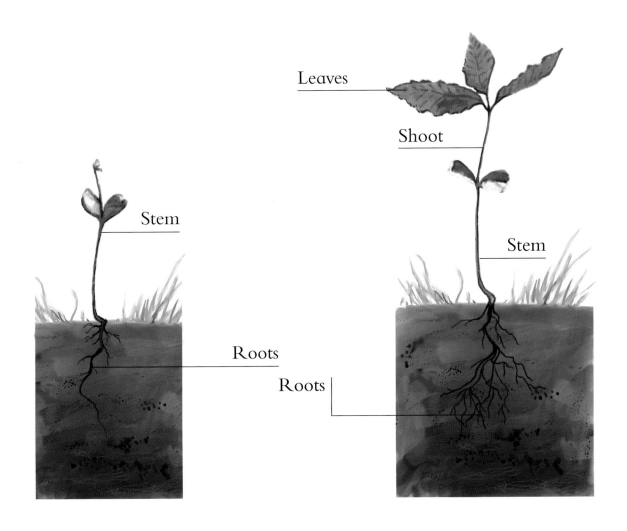

Leaves

Branches

Bark

Trunk

The young tree keeps growing if it gets enough water and sunlight to survive.

In its next year of life, the tree grows buds that may turn into leaves. Soon the tree has branches, a woody trunk, bark, and lots of leaves.

Each year, the tree grows taller, and its trunk gets wider.
A forester can tell how old a tree is by counting its rings.
A tree trunk has one ring for each year it has been alive.
This tree was more than a hundred years old.

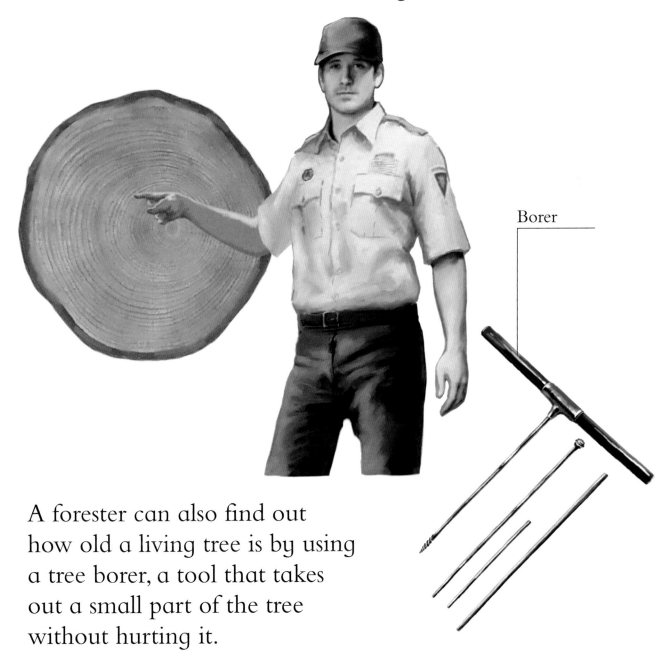

Borer

A forester can also find out
how old a living tree is by using
a tree borer, a tool that takes
out a small part of the tree
without hurting it.

9

After our trip to the forest, I wanted to grow
a tree of my own. Dad took me to a nursery,
where you can buy flowers, shrubs, and trees.

A nursery has trees that have grown big enough to transplant, or plant in a new place.

The nursery worker showed me trees that have flowers in the spring and fruit in the summer. We looked at trees with soft leaves and trees with pine needles.

I chose a maple tree. My tree was already more than four feet high, just a little taller than me.

The nursery worker helped us choose a shovel to plant the tree. She recommended organic fertilizer to feed the tree as it grew.

Then she went over the instructions on how to plant my tree.

I picked out a place in our backyard where the tree would have lots of sunlight and lots of room to grow.

Then, Dad and I dug a hole with the shovel.
The hole was as deep as the tree's root ball
and about three times as wide.

We carefully lowered the tree into the hole. We loosened the burlap bag around the roots.

Next, we filled in soil around the tree. I added organic fertilizer to the soil and sprinkled mulch on top.

Then I gave my tree a nice drink of water.

Dad asked an arborist to check the other trees in our yard. An arborist is like a doctor for trees. She pruned the branches of our big trees with pruning shears.

She checked all
the trees for signs
of disease. She also
listened for bugs
by using a stethoscope.
She looked like
a doctor!

One of our oldest
trees had been
damaged in a storm.
The arborist used
a handsaw and a
chain saw to cut
off two broken limbs.

I asked the arborist to check my tree.
She said it was doing just fine. She
added a stake to help it grow up straight.

When the weather turned cold, my tree's green leaves
turned bright red. Then they twirled down to the ground.

The next spring, my tree grew buds that turned
into leaves. Over the summer, it grew branches
with more leaves. Its trunk grew thicker.

Close-up of red maple
branch with buds
on in the spring

This is a leaf from my red maple tree.
It has three lobes that have saw-toothed edges.

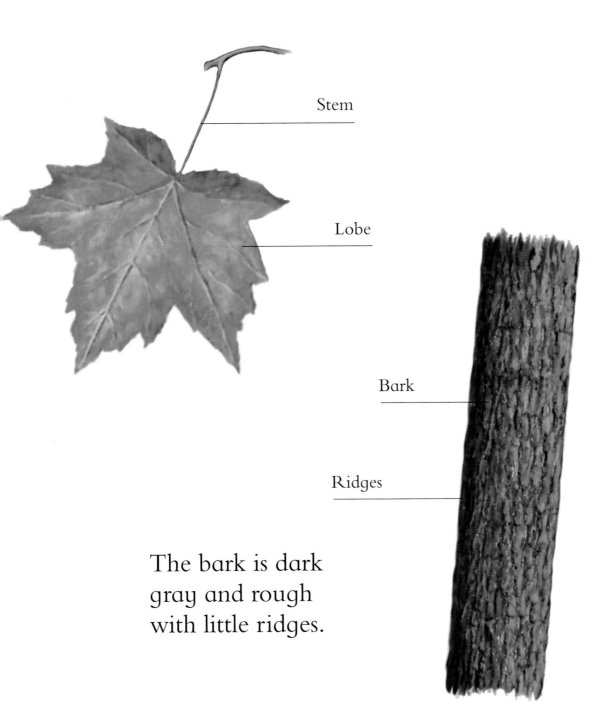

Stem

Lobe

Bark

Ridges

The bark is dark
gray and rough
with little ridges.

All summer, I watered my tree and checked it for insects. It just kept growing!

The arborist said that my tree could grow 60 feet high. That's taller than my house.

Look at my tree now.
It's much taller than
I am. If I take good
care of it, it will be
around for a long,
long time.

A tree is a great
friend to grow
up with.

You can plant a tree, too.
Which tree would you choose?

Oak

Palm

Pine

Weeping Willow

Japanese Maple

Sweet Cherry